Improve Your Life

Simple Ways to Live the Life you Want

SUCCESS
ESTEEM   BELIEF
CALMNESS   ASSURANCE
CONFIDENCE   POSITIVITY
EMPOWERMENT   RELAXATION

Janice Johnson

authorHOUSE®

AuthorHouse™ UK
1663 Liberty Drive
Bloomington, IN 47403 USA
www.authorhouse.co.uk
Phone: 0800.197.4150

© 2016 Janice Johnson. All rights reserved.

No part of this book may be reproduced, stored in a retrieval system, or transmitted by any means without the written permission of the author.

Published by AuthorHouse 06/10/2016

ISBN: 978-1-5246-3502-2 (sc)
ISBN: 978-1-5246-3503-9 (e)

Print information available on the last page.

Any people depicted in stock imagery provided by Thinkstock are models, and such images are being used for illustrative purposes only. Certain stock imagery © Thinkstock.

This book is printed on acid-free paper.

Because of the dynamic nature of the Internet, any web addresses or links contained in this book may have changed since publication and may no longer be valid. The views expressed in this work are solely those of the author and do not necessarily reflect the views of the publisher, and the publisher hereby disclaims any responsibility for them.

AUTHOR'S NOTE

On the cover of this book you will see inspirational words in the form of a bridge.

I have a fondness for bridges and like to look at and appreciate them. I also see bridges as a link between how you are now and how you want to be.

As you come across bridges in your everyday life think about your journey.

Appreciate the progress you have made and the steps you have taken. Some of them will have been difficult, some smoother and easier and others hard to overcome. Looking back you can appreciate your progress.

Developing the person you wish to be and the life you wish to lead is your transition from one side of the bridge to the other. Each step represents what you gain, experience, and learn to leave behind.

Also included are inspirational quotations. These are to encourage you, give you, the reader, something to think about and also to support the content.

And if I repeat myself it is simply to reinforce the message.

There are elements of our lives about which we can do little, but there will be aspects that can be changed and improved which will create a happier and more rewarding life.

ACKNOWLEDGEMENTS

This book benefitted from the following contributions:

Glenys for her support and proof reading skills which helped to make this book the best it could be.

Sandra for reviewing the material, giving me encouragement and always believing in me.

Finally to my family, Peter, Nicola, Helen, Joanne, Nick, Aaron and Ian for their never ending love which I cherish.

My love and appreciation to you all.

I woke up one morning

and never looked back.

INTRODUCTION

This book contains my experience, and that of working with clients, plus lots of proven ways to help you make a difference to your life.

The most difficult part of making any changes is the decision to do so, and then taking the necessary action.

Often we will put this off by hoping things will get better or putting the blame on to other people. It would be so easy if someone could wave a magic wand over us, but this would mean missing out on your developing self.

Gradually we come to the realisation that there is only one person that can put things right, and that is ourselves.

'I wanted to discover ....
that bit of fibre which can be developed in all of us –
there it is – waiting to be used.

Katharine Hepburn
Me: Stories of my life

I see this fibre as our core of determination, motivation and inner strength that we can draw on and use to our advantage.

Be passionate about yourself and the life you desire and find the fibre waiting inside you to be used for this purpose.

WHAT THIS BOOK WILL DO FOR YOU

The aim of this book is to help you achieve the following.

To learn ways in which you can make positive changes to improve your life by –

>Building confidence
>Raising self-esteem
>Increasing self-belief
>Setting achievable goals
>Using positive affirmations
>Visualisation to create powerful images
>Empowerment
>Gaining self-assurance
>Relaxation
>Learning skills for the future
>Achieving success

FACT

What you put into your mind is what comes out of it.

GOOD IDEA

Focus on what you want and how you want life to be.

WHO OR WHAT IS DRIVING YOUR LIFE?

Are you in the driving seat of your life or are you a passenger?

Are you in charge of where you are going?

Do you have a journey in mind or are you aimlessly moving through life?

It is OK to be a passenger as long as you are happy and content with where life is leading you.

But is someone else making decisions about your life, based on what they think you should be doing?

This book can help you focus and take more control.

The simple ideas contained herein can help you improve your life and how you live it.

This book can help to give you greater fulfilment and contentment. It can help you focus on what is important and to let go of what is no longer needed. It can help you sort things out and deal with matters that hinder you.

This book can also help you to find the life you want to live and help you create a brighter future and a happier tomorrow.

Love the life you live
Live the life you love

Bob Marley

MIND-BODY CONNECTION

The language used to refer to yourself is of real importance. The mind-body connection organises itself around verbal experiences.

Words can either be a tool to help or a weapon to hurt.

Think about the kind of subliminal messages you give yourself, for example,

> 'I can't do that, I'm useless'
> 'I'm too old'.

Destructive thinking creates blockages and blockages are stagnant energy which has an effect on your health and well-being.

Your cells, as they die, pass on these negative messages and as your cells are constantly renewing themselves they receive these comments.

You make

> a new liver every six weeks
> a new stomach lining every five days
> new skin once a month and
> even your brain cells are new from last year.

When we take responsibility and release the negative blockages and create uplifting and inspiring thoughts and beliefs, our life can be transformed and we can heal ourselves.

SELF HELP

From what clients have said and from my own personal experience I know how vulnerable we are as human beings. Destructive thoughts play a major role. Because we are continually thinking, so we are continually constructing.

We want to be liked. We want to receive approval.

The media promote ideas, especially in magazines, devoted to what we eat, wear, say and do. So we are far more conscious of our appearance and behaviour.

Despite the proliferation of self-help books and the numerous articles in magazines and journals we can still remain the same.

All this knowledge does help in providing awareness and giving us ideas.

But what stops us from putting them into practise?

Sometimes we can tell ourselves it is too difficult. Maybe it is, but it isn't too difficult.

By choosing to do things that aren't easy, we grow as people and feel good about our achievements.

So do something for you and help yourself now.

What you resist persists

Carl Jung

LOVING YOURSELF

This chapter will enable you to identify ways in which you have been less than loving towards yourself. It will give examples of how you can put more love back into your life and so become more loving towards yourself and others.

**Once you have learned to love,
you will have learned to live.**

Love is your foundation for living. It improves:

Self-esteem
Self-confidence
Self-worth
Self-assurance
Self-approval
Self-respect
Self-regard
Self-appreciation
Self-fulfilment
Self-knowledge

It is no coincidence that these all begin with 'self' because it is you that generates the feelings and emotions that create your self-image, your sense of self, and how you view yourself in relation to your world.

WHO IS SELF?

It is the 'you' that is; that exists. Self is the individual with a character and personality that is uniquely yours and which identifies you. Self is the person with a history. Self is the 'I', the ego that is conscious and thinks.

THE VOICE OF A CHILD

I need the you, that is now, to provide.
My needs are simple, they are yours
I need love
I need respect
I need you to understand who I am
to remember, I am you.

L Foulkes

HOW YOU FEEL ABOUT YOURSELF IS IMPORTANT

Negative messages from yourself or other people condition your perceptions. If continuously reinforced, these messages will affect how you feel about yourself.

When you feel good about yourself, you will see other's behaviour, if directed against you, as their problem.

DO YOU LOVE YOURSELF?

It is amazing how many people, when asked if they love themselves, say "no". Or if asked how they feel about themselves, give a negative answer.

Loving yourself is the foundation from which you build a strong base to create the life you want and the person you want to be.

Improve Your Life

ABOUT ME

Not long ago I reached a time in my life where I was totally exhausted. I felt worn out, worn down and tired.

People told me to look after myself. I thought about this phrase, 'look after myself'. What did it mean?

As a wife, mother and therapist I was looking after others but along the way I had stopped looking after me. I had forgotten to give myself time and attention.

I HAD FORGOTTEN TO LOVE AND CARE FOR MYSELF

Having no time isn't a reason, it is an excuse.

'An excuse is a person's refusal to take responsibility for a decision they've already made not to do something.'

Cliff Stockamp

Now I needed time. Self knowledge comes with spending time with yourself. As you begin to know yourself better you can stop acting out unnecessary roles, challenge your assumptions, take control of your life, change habits and beliefs, become more selective and learn to say 'no' to others and 'yes' to yourself.

My work was important to me so making the decision to take time out for me was difficult and yet, once made, became an enormous relief.

SO WHAT HAPPENED?

I had ignored my own philosophy. Clients were entreated to love themselves physically, mentally, emotionally and spiritually but I had stopped following my own advice. Physically I had pushed myself too much and my spirit was low. I had taken from myself but not put back into myself.

REMEMBER

It's not what happens to you, it's what you do about it.

SO I DID SOMETHING
WILL YOU?

DEFINITION OF LOVE

Love is many things; it is multi-faceted. The following are just some of the examples I came up with. Maybe you can add to this list?
Love is the energy that drives you.
Love is the fuel that warms your heart and soul.
Love heals.
Love lights you up from the inside.
Love is the ability to forgive.
Love sets you free.
Love is giving you the care and consideration you deserve.
Love is not only words but also actions.
Love is the ability to give to yourself and be able to freely receive from you.
Love is enabling you to feel special – and so you are.
Love is feeling good about yourself even when people are telling you you're bad.

Improve Your Life

Love is compassion and kindness.
Love is quiet. Love is gentle. Love is soft.

IT'S AMAZING THE IMPACT LOVE CAN HAVE ON THE BODY

In his book Quantum Healing, Dr Deepak Chopra tells a powerful story about the connection between love and physical healing:

> *"An Ohio University study of heart disease in the 1970s was conducted by feeding quite toxic, high-cholesterol diets to rabbits in order to block their arteries, duplicating the effect that such a diet has on human arteries. Consistent results began to appear in all the rabbit groups except for one, which strangely displayed 60 per cent fewer symptoms. Nothing in the rabbits' physiology could account for their high tolerance to the diet, until it was discovered by accident that the student who was in charge of feeding these particular rabbits liked to fondle and pet them. He would hold each rabbit lovingly for a few minutes before feeding it; astonishingly, this alone seemed to enable the animals to overcome the toxic diet. Repeat experiments, in which one group of rabbits was treated neutrally while the others were loved, came up with similar results."*

TALKING ABOUT BODIES

Do you criticise your body for what it isn't rather than praise it for what it is?

Alienating and rejecting your body is felt inwardly. Would you say such hurtful comments to anyone other than yourself? No. So why say them to you. All you are doing is hurting yourself. Stop it now.

Start loving your body just as it is. Pamper yourself with a facial, a massage, or an aromatherapy bath. Eat more healthily and take exercise. Generally take more interest in your body and give it loving attention.

Then perhaps like the rabbits in the above story you may become more resistant to illness and disease.

YOU ARE WHAT YOU THINK

*'There is nothing either good or bad,
but thinking makes it so.'*

William Shakespeare

Change your thoughts and notice how you are able to change your life.

'Our life is what our thoughts make it.'

Marcus Aurelius

YOUR OPINIONS MATTER

You receive these opinions in various ways. For instance, through negative self-talk. This is the inner dialogue that is constantly going on in your head. Also the way you put yourself down when talking to other people. By focusing on your 'lack of'. Judging yourself as not being good enough. Criticising what you do and how you do things and highlighting what you ought to have done and haven't. Negative thinking and belittling beliefs.

Your beliefs programme you. A belief is something that you accept as true. But what are these limiting beliefs costing you?

For example:

"I'm not very good at this sort of thing."
"Trust me to get it wrong."
"I may not be able to do it."
"I'm useless."

Stop using this kind of damaging dialogue and replace such phrases with something more supportive and creative that will build you up instead of knocking you down.

For example:

"With practice I can improve."
"I'll have a go."
"I can do some things better than others."

WORDS HAVE TREMENDOUS POWER – THEY CAN EITHER BE TOOLS OR WEAPONS

The way you use words can either be constructive or destructive. Stop and think about any destructive words you may use towards yourself.

What you tell yourself has an impact on your life. So choose words that empower you and make you feel good.

Through awareness and observation comes change and transformation.

DEVELOP AN AWARENESS

Notice what you say and think. This will happen gradually. Don't judge these words or thoughts – just become aware of them. Then start to eliminate them and replace them with more empowering words. Give yourself lots of encouragement and notice the difference.

BE KIND TO YOURSELF

*'You are your own best friend;
so be kind to yourself.'*

Vera Peiffer

So give yourself praise rather than criticism. Criticism reinforces the feeling of not being good enough. How can you be good enough when you judge yourself in a negative way?

WHAT ELSE AFFECTS US?

Early conditioning or imprinting, for example, 'Children should be seen and not heard'. In childhood we are at our most impressionable. Attitudes are passed on to us from family, peers and society. Are you still maintaining and reinforcing the negative messages you received as a child? What behaviour have you picked up? Have you learned how to be anxious or to feel depressed?

Improve Your Life

Expectations – yours or other peoples? Are they attainable or out of your reach – thereby enforcing a sense of failure or of not being good enough? If repeated, the effects will be reinforced.

Wanting approval, otherwise known as the disease to please. It matters what people think about us. We care about what they say about us. We fear rejection.

Guilt, blame, fear, and anxiety. We can spend too much time either regretting the past or anticipating the future. We miss out on not being in the present moment – the here and now.

WELCOME MISTAKES

We all make mistakes and this is how we learn. Each mistake builds on the last and is part of the experience of learning. This kind of learning is creative, building blocks of knowledge that keep growing and developing over time.

Think of a child that is learning to walk. Does it give up just because it falls over? No. It keeps on trying and most likely you encourage the child until it succeeds in walking. Do you tell the child off for falling? No. You praise its tenacity.

So falling down isn't failure; it is part of success and how you learn to get up and stay up.

STOP BLAMING AND CRITICISING

We blame and criticise others for the way they treat us and for the things they do to us. But it is nothing compared to what we can say and do to ourselves.

> 'Your road is paved with gold.
> So why do you only see concrete?'

APPROVAL AND APPRECIATION

We have the ability to give ourselves the approval and appreciation to feel valued.

When we give to ourselves we will no longer be looking outside of ourselves for others to provide what we need.

We stop being a needy person because we are now meeting our own needs. When others show us love, respect, kindness and compassion it is a bonus.

So by giving ourselves approval and appreciation we no longer search for others to fulfil these expressions of worth.

This is what loving ourselves is all about.

> 'He who seeks for applause only from without
> has all his happiness in another's keeping.
>
> *Oliver Goldsmith*

UNCONDITIONAL LOVE

Love without any expectations can make a major positive impact on the whole course of your life.

LOVE IS THE ABILITY TO FORGIVE

Love is the ability to forgive: either yourself or others. Why? Because forgiveness frees you from the chains of past events, situations and people.

Forgiveness enables you to let go of the past, which is keeping you locked into the past and so enables you to move forward into the present.

People do what they do and say what they say with the knowledge and experience they have at the time. We are all experts in retrospect.

When we know better we do better.

Forgive others their faults just as <u>you</u> can forgive your own.

START GIVING YOURSELF ATTENTION

Sometimes we put ourselves last and ignore our own wishes and desires, maybe to show just how magnanimous we can be.

It's great to do things for other people.

<u>But what about you?</u>

Your spirit is crying out for attention. Your heart wants to beat with joy.

I know that when I give myself the care and consideration that I deserve everything in life picks up as a consequence and I feel happier and healthier.

SO WHAT'S STOPPING YOU?

The voice of the ego stirs up fear, guilt and blame and so on. It delves into the past to bring up examples of our failure and projects into the future creating anxiety.

Emotions such as defeat and depression stop you from doing those things that can change your life.

Sometimes it can be uncomfortable, even frightening, to change. Maybe it is difficult also but aren't you worth it?

FEAR IS A RUNAWAY TRAIN

Fear of the future, fear of change and even fear of not really knowing what to do, can keep us stuck.

Fear destroys confidence and stops us moving on.

Fear breeds fear.

Fear can create anxiety, worry and depression.

Fear can erode self-esteem.

LOOK AT FEAR ANOTHER WAY

Marianne Williamson helps us to perceive fear in another way.

"Our deepest fear is not that we are inadequate
Our deepest fear is that we are powerful beyond measure
It is our light, not our darkness, that most frightens us.
We ask ourselves:
'Who am I to be brilliant, gorgeous, talented, fabulous?'
Actually, who are you not to be?
You are a child of God.
Your playing small doesn't serve the world.

Marianne Williamson
'A Return to Love'

IS YOUR CUP FULL AND RUNNING OVER?

As a child I went to Sunday school and there we sang a song, which went:

"My cup's full and running over …"

This sums up what we can do for ourselves. Your cup, the vessel that is you, can be filled to overflowing with love and kindness.

The love you give to yourself is just as important and perhaps even more than the love others give you.

GO WITHIN

*'If you fail to go within,
you will go without.'*

Neil Donald Walsh

So direct attention inwards. Start giving to yourself. Don't look out there. Look within.

*Man struggles to find life outside himself,
unaware that the life he is seeking is within him.*

*Kahlil Gibran
(The Prophet)*

FILL UP YOUR CUP

So how can you 'fill up your cup'? There are various ways, some of which are listed below:

Be kind to yourself
Stop running yourself down
Give yourself lots of praise, support and encouragement
Put joy into your life
Do things that bring you happiness
Smile more
Enjoy what you have
Appreciate the person you are
Adopt an attitude of gratitude
Treat yourself

LOOK AT IT THIS WAY

Another way is to think of all the 'self' words and begin to actualise them. Words such as the following:

Self-approval – stop criticising and judging yourself too harshly.
Self-appreciation – compliment yourself on how you look and what you do.
Self-assurance – be positive about yourself, smile, hold your head up and shoulders back.
Self-esteem – always acknowledge your achievements however small.
Self-regard – remember to talk about yourself in positive terms.
Self-respect – honour the person you are and don't put yourself down.
Self-confidence – believe in yourself and your abilities.

BELIEFS

Beliefs have a major impact on our lives. They underpin our perceptions. A belief is something you accept as being true. However, it may be imagination. If we think something often enough we can convince ourselves it is true.

'A lie unchallenged becomes the truth'

By taking a reality check and asking yourself if it is real then you can halt the process, the pattern or habit. Then ask yourself what is really true and what you want to be true.

BELIEVE IN WHAT YOU WANT

Beliefs programme us and create our self-image, environment and our place in the world.

'Truly, whatever the mind can conceive and believe, the mind can achieve.'

Napoleon Hill

So when we change our beliefs to those we want and which will enhance our life, we set off a chain reaction. The new beliefs will then influence our thinking, that chatter which goes on in our heads and sometimes seems relentless.

THOUGHTS

Thoughts maintain and express our beliefs. When you change what you say, whether to yourself (self-talk) or others, you will begin to change your feelings, thoughts and behaviour.

beliefs
↓
influence
↓
thoughts
↓
influence
↓
behaviour

So from this you will see that if you change your beliefs, you will change the influence they have on your thinking

Improve Your Life | 21

and ultimately will change the influence they have on your behaviour. Consequently you will feel better about yourself and your life.

Have you ever wondered why you sometimes reject compliments? It is because they don't match your beliefs.

PUT IT INTO PRACTICE

*'They always say time changes things,
but you actually have to change them yourself.'*

Andy Warhol

For example, if you act as if you were not 'good enough' your behaviour will reflect this belief.

So write down what your negative beliefs are now, and then, based on these beliefs, write down what you want to believe.

As an example, if your present belief is "I am not good enough".

Your new belief would be "I am good enough".

NOW CHANGE YOUR THINKING

Look at how you can influence your thinking to support this new belief. Well for one thing you would stop being critical.

Start to empower yourself with positive comments that prove you are 'good enough'.

Such as

"I wrote a letter today and was able to express myself really well".
"I like the way I am handling my life now".
"This colour suits me".
"It is amazing what I can do".
"I feel better about myself".

Now that you are starting to think well of yourself how can you reflect these new beliefs in the way you behave?

Become aware of your interactions with other people. These will give you a clue.

'The only thing in the world you can change is yourself and that makes all the difference in the world.'

Cher

SO WHAT ARE YOU WAITING FOR?

When you get up each morning ask yourself, "What am I going to do for me today?" It doesn't have to be big or major, although sometimes it can be.

Small things can be just as powerful in the effect they have on you.

At the end of the day ask yourself what have you enjoyed about your day and what has made you happy?

For example, I am writing this during springtime and I have a lot of pleasure looking at the buds bursting into life. I enjoy the colours and perfumes of the spring flowers and the song of the birds.

PASS LOVE ON

Having learned how important it is for us to feel the expression of love we are then able to pass on love to others.

Also it has a boomerang effect. What you give out comes back.

Here is an example of how love can make a difference to other people's lives. It is written by Eric Butterworth in the book "Chicken Soup for the Soul".

> *'A college professor had his sociology class go into the Baltimore slums to get case histories of 200 young boys. They were asked to write an evaluation of each boy's future. In every case the students wrote, "He hasn't got a chance." Twenty-five years later another sociology professor came across the earlier study. He had his students follow up on the project to see what had happened to these boys. With the exception of 20 boys, who had moved away or died, the students learned that 176 of the remaining 180 had achieved more than ordinary success as lawyers, doctors and businessmen.*
>
> *The professor was astounded and decided to pursue the matter further. Fortunately, all the men were in the area and he was able to ask each one, "How do you account for your success?". In each case the reply came with feeling, "There was a teacher."*

The teacher was still alive, so he sought her out and asked the old but still alert lady what magic formula she had used to pull these boys out of the slums into successful achievement.

The teacher's eyes sparkled and her lips broke into a gentle smile. "It's really very simple," she said. "I loved those boys."

HOW WILL YOU FEEL?

Hurt, sorrow and anger begin to have less of a part in your life. You no longer inflict them on others or yourself.

Your inner self is well fed and no longer starved of love and attention. The empty feeling has gone.

Remember that feeling of comfort after you have just eaten a very satisfying and filling meal? This is the contentment and peace you will feel.

DOES IT HAPPEN OVERNIGHT?

No. Working on you takes time and effort. Changing perceptions and patterns of thinking and behaviour takes time and perseverance. You are worth it though.

The man who removes a mountain begins by carrying small stones.

Chinese Proverb

Don't be put off because

> LOVING YOURSELF **CAN** BEGIN
> TO HAPPEN IMMEDIATELY

All it takes is a willingness on your part to invest time and effort in transforming you and your life.

> *'When you change the way you look at things,*
> *the things you look at change.'*

GOOD IDEA

Stop trying to go forward whilst still looking backwards.

FACT

If you were driving a car you would crash.

THE WAY OUT OF DEPRESSION

The type of depression referred to here is reactive depression. This means reacting to what is going on around you such as with people, events, your environment and the feelings and perceptions you have towards yourself.

The ideas given here are not to resolve the more serious forms of depression but they may help to alleviate some symptoms.

Feeling down and depressed often takes us within ourselves. It's like retreating from the outside world although there is still a lot going on mentally. Often there is also a withdrawal from activities previously enjoyed. All of this reinforces the depressive state.

People involve in negative introspection by becoming more critical, often judging themselves as not good enough. Negative and distorted thinking is characteristic of depression. We can have feelings of being trapped in a situation and can't see a way out.

Sometimes thinking can have the three 'p' effect:

Personal – a negative view as in 'I'm no good' or 'I'll never do it'

Pervasive – widespread and universal as in 'Everything is against me' or 'I'm useless at everything'

Perpetual – long-lasting and forever as in 'I'll never get over this' or 'I shall be like this forever'.

Researchers have found that depression is associated with memory bias. This means having a poorer memory for positive events and experiences and therefore a better memory for negative happenings.

Other effects can include loss of pleasure, interest, libido, appetite, poor sleep, indecisiveness, suicidal thoughts, and feelings of sadness, lack of energy, utter fatigue, restlessness and agitation.

Sadness and feeling low are different to depression and it is important to distinguish the difference.

A trigger is often around emotional needs not being met and also a loss of control.

Women suffer depression more than men. This could be because women are more in tune with their emotions or due to the different pressures they have juggling home, children, work and social life.

Another way of looking at depression is as a way of drawing our attention to something that needs fixing or sorting out.

Motivation becomes a problem because generally this comes before action.

Indeed it is a good antidote for the depressed person to come up with solutions or answers to their problems. Action forces the person to disrupt their cycle of depressive-inducing thinking.

What to do?

Controlling depressive thoughts and beliefs helps to overcome feelings of helplessness and hopelessness.

Phrase things more positively and use optimistic language whenever possible.

Find solutions to problems instead of worrying about them.

Direct attention outwards.

Regain interest in things outside of yourself.

See friends and arrange outings. Push yourself to do things.

Do the things you enjoy doing.

Regular activity helps to improve energy and mood levels. Walking is ideal or being involved in some sort of outdoor activity.

Take a holiday or weekend away.

Notice good things.

Change perspectives and look at things differently.

Keep focused on the present and stop lingering on negative past issues as experiences condition us and looking back reconditions bad thoughts and depressive feelings.

Be more realistic in expectations of yourself and others.

Acknowledge your achievements and aspire to do more to help yourself.

Maybe join a gym or class.

Exercise and doing things you enjoy release endorphins which boost your feel good factor.

Watch comedy or read humorous stories.

Treat yourself even if it's a bunch of flowers or a book or magazine.

Having a massage will help you feel good.

Talking therapies such as psychotherapy or counselling have their own way of helping.

Learn to relax or meditate as this helps to calm emotions and heightened feelings.

Hypnotherapy can help to solve those problems that won't go away.

FACT

Imagination is powerful but it isn't real.
Negatively it can cause a fearful future. Positively
it can create inspiration and motivation.

GOOD IDEA

Do a reality check. Are you creating a 'what if'
scenario or visualising things going wrong? Ask yourself
if what you are thinking is real or is it happening
now. If the answer is 'no' then stop that thought.

PANIC ATTACKS

So overwhelming are the symptoms of panic attacks that some people believe they are experiencing a heart attack.

Panic attacks are the inappropriate activation of the fight or flight response. The person concerned is responding to fear or perceiving a situation as dangerous to them. They occur when there is a build up of stress that the person cannot cope with any longer.

Symptoms are a pounding heart, sweating and rapid breathing, and feeling faint. These symptoms cause even more panic which releases more adrenaline and this continues increasing the reactions; fear of the fear.

Sometimes wherever the panic attack is experienced becomes a place of fear, and is then linked together. It could happen in a supermarket or a train station. The person would then avoid going into these places feeling they are responsible for the panic attack.

This avoidance creates a phobia. Other environments may be added.

The answer:

Relaxation to calm the nerves and reduce anxiety.

Realising that it is what is happening inside that causes the response.

Look at what is creating the stress response or the thoughts and beliefs that manifest the fear. What is the trigger?

Look at ways of dealing with the problem. Ask for help if necessary.

Avoid using words like fear, anxiety or worry in relation to this situation.

Imagine going into the place or places that are avoided in a calm and relaxed manner. Then go there in reality by breaking the visits down into manageable and achievable goals. Don't rush this phase.

Give lots of reassurance that everything will be ok.

FACT

The longer you hold on to a burden
the heavier it becomes.

GOOD IDEA

Put it down and do something about it.

PEACE OF MIND

If you are anything like me there are times when your mind seems to have a will of its own. I have learned that you can control your mind. Yes, it is difficult and yes, you do have to practise. But peace of mind can be yours.

WHAT IS IT?

It is the element of a person that enables them to be aware of the world and their experiences, to think, reason and to feel; the faculty of consciousness and thought.

WHERE IS IT?

Scientists agree that they have yet to discover where the mind is! Its location remains a mystery.

IS THE MIND PART OF THE BRAIN?

Confusion can arise on the question of where the mind is located and sometimes it can be thought of as being part of the brain. However, because the brain is a physical object it can be seen and felt, whereas the mind cannot be seen or felt because it isn't a physical object.

*To a mind that is still
the whole universe surrenders.*

Chuang Tzu

SO WHERE IS IT?

If we don't know what the mind is, then it is difficult to know where to find it. So, does God have the answer?

In his book 'Conversations with God' Book 3, Neale Donald Walsch has a dialogue with God on the subject. He is told that our mind is not in our head; it is in every cell of our body. As there are more cells in your brain than anywhere else, is why it seems as if the mind is there.

God explains, *"What you call the mind is really an energy. It is thought. And thought is energy, not an object. Your brain is an object. It is a physical, biochemical mechanism – the largest, most sophisticated, but not the only mechanism in the human body, with which the body translates, or converts, the energy which is your thought into physical impulses. Your brain is a transformer. So is your whole body. You have little transformers in every cell. Biochemists have often remarked at how individual cells seem to have their own intelligence."*

THE BUDDHIST VIEW

A good explanation is given by Geshe Kelsang Gyatso in his book 'Introduction to Buddhism', where he describes the mind as a 'formless continuum that functions to perceive and understand objects'. He says that it would be impossible for the body to go to the moon without travelling in a spaceship whereas our mind can reach the moon instantly just by thinking about it.

"In the Buddhist scriptures our body is compared to a guest house and our mind to a guest dwelling within it. When we

die our mind leaves our body and goes to the next life, just like a guest leaving a guesthouse and going somewhere else."

IMPACT

Irrespective of what it is or where it is, what we do know is that the mind can be very powerful and have a major impact on our health and well-being.

WHAT DOES PEACE OF MIND MEAN TO YOU?

I asked various people that very question and here are their answers.

To know my family are safe and happy.
Knowing that my husband and I are okay.
Having a comfortable living.
Freedom.
Everything I think about is in order.
Being at ease with the world and myself.
Having a clear conscience.
To be loved.
Enough money.
You feel you have done your best.
Paying off a debt – either financial or moral.
Not having to worry.
Making wise decisions
Carefree

Maybe you can add to this list and think about what gives you peace of mind. Just giving your attention to the subject will increase your awareness. Remember - you always get more of what you focus on.

DICTIONARY DEFINITION

The Chambers English Dictionary states that the mind means:

Memory; record; that which thinks, knows, feels and wills; soul; personality; seat of consciousness, thought, volition and feeling.

The Penguin Dictionary of Psychology describes the mind as – 'the battered offspring of the union of philosophy and psychology'.

History reveals two conflicting impulses; the tendencies to either treat the mind as a metaphysical or biological entity.

Deep in the centre of each of us is a pool of peace.

Diana Cooper

Let this book help you to find your peace of mind.

SOPHIA LOREN

Once when Sophia Loren was visiting New York, burglars broke into her hotel suite and demanded her jewellery. They threatened to kill her children if she did not comply. There was no choice. She had to open the safe and give them the jewels.

Although upset by the incident, nevertheless her motto in life is 'never to cry over things that cannot cry over you'.

She says that positive thinking is an important part of her philosophy on life. What she calls "good thoughts" provide a positive outlook that builds inner strength.

Also when cooking she says she is able to find the peace of mind that previously seemed to have gone away.

LOOKING BACK

In interviews with the elderly and the terminally ill, people talk about the things they regret not having done.

Even now some of you are probably already thinking about the things you would like to do. Don't keep putting them off.

DO THEM NOW.

IF I HAD MY LIFE TO LIVE OVER

I'd dare to make more mistakes next time.
I'd relax. I would limber up.
I would perhaps have more actual troubles
but I'd have fewer imaginary ones.
You see, I'm one of those people who live sensibly
and sanely hour after hour, day after day.
Oh, I've had my moments and if I had it to
do over again, I'd have more of them.
One after another, instead of living so
many years ahead of each day.
Nadine Stair (age 85 years)

BE PRESENT

Your mind will often take you back into the past using memory. Or, alternatively, project you into the future using imagination. Life can only be lived in the present.

THE POWER OF NOW

Eckhart Tolle has written a book called the 'Power of Now' in which he advocates that we live in the 'now' moment. Not the past or the future but now. He states that we can always cope with the 'now', but never with the future, and nor do we have to because the answer, the strength, the right action or resource, will be there when we need it, not before, and not after.

So ask yourself the question "What problem do I have right now?" - not next week or next month.

We need time to be
not do or say anything
just to be
even if it is only for a minute or two.
Once you experience the benefits of just being
you will never look back.

IMAGINARY TROUBLES

It's a fact that many of us spend time saying "What if ...?" But how often does the 'what if' actually happen? Look at the energy we burn up pondering this question. Look at how much anxiety and stress we create!

Do we worry about running out of bread or milk next week? No, because we know that if we do run out, we go and buy some more.

Although a simple analogy, it does hold the key to the question. Action is the answer.

When you ponder a question, take it one step further and find the answer. Don't leave questions hanging in mid air, unanswered.

Come up with a solution and take action.

FUTURE PROJECTION

The problems arise when questions are future based. We cannot solve anything that hasn't happened. As yet the future is an illusion. So when we project into the future with a 'what if' question that cannot be answered, we create anxiety. Then we remain anxious waiting for whatever it is to happen.

IN THE MIND

Our minds may remind us of past indiscretions and failures. The future may be fraught with obstacles as our minds fill us with fear-ridden messages but Patrick Holford and Dr Hyla Cass write in their book 'Natural Highs' that most stressors are not disasters. Thinking they are however can easily overwhelm you.

TO BE MIND FREE

In his book 'Practising the Power of Now' Eckhart Tolle says, "The moment that judgement stops through acceptance of what is, you are free of the mind".

There is a silence into which the world cannot intrude.
There is an ancient peace you carry in
your heart and have not lost.

From "A Course in Miracles"

SIGN OF PEACE

These days ministers invite their congregation to give each other a sign of peace. This can be a smile, handshake, or a hug. During this exchange the words "Peace be with you" are spoken to each recipient.

Wouldn't this be a wonderful way of passing on peace?

MEDITATION

The purpose of meditation is to calm the mind, relax the body and give a feeling of inner peace whilst remaining focused and aware.

Meditation will also quieten the brain waves and lower blood pressure.

It is easy to begin and can become more advanced as you progress. There are many books on the subject and finding the right one for you is a personal choice.

Similarly, joining a meditation group is going to be relative to your needs. It is all about what is right for you. If you aren't sure, then it is worth sampling to find out.

Enjoy the journey.

DON'T BE PUT OFF

Sometimes, though, there can be pre-conceptions about meditation that can make it appear more difficult than it actually is.

We may also use lack of time as an excuse for not starting.

Remember, peace of mind can be yours for just a few minutes a day.

Listen in deep silence.
Be very still and open your mind ...
Sink deep into the peace that waits for you
beyond the frantic riotous thoughts and
sights and sounds of this insane world.

From "A Course in Miracles"

TO GET STARTED

Starting can be as easy as stopping what you're doing, closing your eyes and focusing your attention on taking a few slow deep breaths.

Controlling the breath is a prerequisite
to controlling the mind and body.

Swami Rama

Or you may want to find a special place to sit, close your eyes and concentrate on your breathing. Become aware of the breaths coming in and going out. If your attention wanders just bring yourself back by again noticing your breathing. Do this for 2/5 minutes initially, gradually building up to 15/20 minutes. Really the choice is yours.

Meditation can be as formal or informal as you wish.

You can focus on the flame of a candle until your eyes just want to close and you drift into a peaceful state. Then let yourself drift down deeper and deeper.

> *The gift of learning to meditate is the greatest gift you can give yourself in this life.*
>
> (Sogyal Rinpoche)

BUSY MIND

Sometimes it can be hard to still the constant chatter that engages our mind. That's fine. Eventually it will happen.

When you are focusing internally, naturally you will become more aware of just how busy your mind can be. Practice is the key.

DON'T GIVE UP

Don't give up or tell yourself you can't meditate. To begin with it may seem that all you are doing is constantly trying to still your busy mind. Keep working through this stage until you progress to the silence that is awaiting you after the chatter has ceased.

MEDITATE ON NATURE

Nature is all around us in many forms; trees, plants, flowers, birds, insects. As nature is bountiful there are endless supplies whether you live in towns and cities or in the country.

Let your eyes focus on one item in particular, for example a tree. Notice the colour of the leaves, their shape, their outlines and size, the texture of the bark and any roots that may be visible.

Similarly, if you are looking at a view, look around in detail and use your senses to focus on what you can see, hear, smell and touch. Afterwards be aware of how you feel.

The practice of meditation has a cumulative effect and the benefits can be felt almost immediately – a sense of detachment from the pressures of life and lasting peace of mind

BE MINDFUL

Mindfulness is a process whereby you give your whole attention to whatever you are doing at any given moment. It is a relaxed state of awareness and a form of Zen Buddhist meditation.

Although mindfulness has been around a long time it has recently become more prominent and the practice has gained more recognition.

In his book on 'How to Meditate' Paul Roland says it is so easy to make excuses as to why it isn't the right time or maybe there are lots of other things you need to do instead.

However, it can be as simple as washing your hands. For example, feel the texture of the soap and really take time to look at your hands.

So whether you are preparing a meal, eating, or anything else, give the task your whole attention and again use your senses to become aware of textures, what you see, hear, smell or taste.

Have you noticed that when you are totally absorbed in something, time flies and you have thought of very little else? Concentrating exclusively on what you are doing stills the mental chatter.

MENTAL CHATTER

If, however, you find your thoughts competing for your attention, draw such thoughts in and become involved with them, observing them instead. These thoughts may try to control you, but by staying mindful and not becoming distracted by them, they will lose their power over you.

> *A peaceful pause*
> *in a moment of time*
> *Silence*
> *to feel the inner stillness*
> *and let everything else melt away.*

SIMPLE RELAXATION

If you want to switch off at any time and relax, have a go at the following.

Sit or lie down comfortably.

Take your attention to outside the room and become aware of external sounds and noises.

Then become aware of what you can hear inside the room.

Now take your awareness within. Notice your breathing and the effect it has, such as the rise and fall of your chest, the cool air that enters your lungs and the warm air that is expelled.

Can you feel the beat of your heart?

Notice the heaviness of your body.

Does your abdomen move to the rhythm of your breathing?

Let thoughts drift in and out of your mind.

Don't draw them in and become involved.

Just let the thoughts ebb and flow, in and out.

Enjoy these moments of peace for as long as you want.

Then bring your attention to the room again.

Now once more take your awareness outside of the room.

So, basically, what you are doing is taking your attention outside the room, inside the room and within yourself, eventually coming back out of yourself to the room you are in and then to outside the room again.

The length of time you spend is up to you.

MENTAL CLUTTER

Have a look at the mental clutter in your life. What are you holding on to? What aren't you sorting out?

The following can take away your peace of mind:

Worry	Insecurity	Criticism
Gossip	Correspondence	Upsets
Negativity	Fears	Blame
Inferiority	Grief	Self pity
Doubts	Disappointments	Promises
Expectations	Habits	Phobias
Complaints	Mental chatter	Anger
Resentment	Unresolved issues	Guilt
Loose ends	Bedtime thoughts	Stress
Frustration	Low self esteem	Failure
Pain	Jealousy	Hurt

The above are the opposite of peace of mind. We mentally bombard ourselves with negative feelings and emotions. Storing up unease, discord and anxiety. Holding on instead of letting go.

Isn't it time you looked at how **you** can clear your mental clutter?

SORT IT OUT

"How" you may say? Start by looking at unresolved issues. Can you forgive others or indeed forgive yourself? Is there something it is time to let go of?

What is causing your 'lack of', criticism, anger, fear and worry? Who do you resent? If you are unable to look at these issues and deal with them yourself, what about seeing a therapist who can help you?

Improve Your Life

If this isn't an option, what about reading some self help books such as this one? Maybe you could talk to a sympathetic and supportive friend or relative.

PROBLEMS

These days there is more pressure placed on people to succeed and to prove themselves. People are overloaded with work and concerned about performance, budgets and finances.

COMPLACENCY

It is so easy to sit back and do nothing. But where will that get you? Will it move you out of the situation or keep you stuck?

> *Man struggles to find life*
> *Outside himself,*
> *Unaware that the life he is seeking*
> *is within him.*
>
> *Kahlil Gibran*
> *(The Prophet)*

BE AT PEACE WITH YOURSELF

Peace of mind can be achieved by stilling the mental chatter, the recriminations, the criticism, and so on. Don't put yourself down. Don't look back in judgement. Know that whatever you did or didn't do in the past seemed the right thing to do at the time. In retrospect you may have done things differently but at the time what you did was based on what you knew then. Time and circumstances change. Life skills and knowledge are gained. Experience is lived.

THE MIND IS A TOOL

The mind is a tool. You can train it. You can control it. Unfortunately the mind has a habit of controlling you. How? It takes you over. Little by little it can steal control away from you.

Because the mind feeds off control its very existence depends on it being in charge. So watch out for self-criticism.

Affirm to yourself:

"I love and approve of myself exactly as I am."

The mind is a powerful tool but it can also be a cruel weapon, especially when used against you. Don't let it run amok. Remember, 'as we think so we are'. Be in charge of your thoughts and feelings.

RESISTANCE TO CHANGE

The ego mind will resist change. It will fight for preservation because change signals loss of control. Persevere because you are worth it.

Louise Hay tells us to say to our mind:

"I now choose to believe it is becoming easier for me to make changes."

Remember that thoughts have no power over you unless you choose to believe them.

DEMANDS

We live in a demanding world where not only do others expect a lot from us but we also expect a lot of ourselves. Sometimes these demands can go beyond what we can realistically supply.

So what happens when we have this shortfall? We may turn on others and ourselves. By focusing on the solution you distance yourself from the problem. Make sure your expectations are realistic and achievable.

BLAME

We may blame others for how we are feeling, little realising that it isn't other people that make us angry, resentful, frustrated – it is ourselves.

We might say "You make me feel ...", whereas really we have created the emotion but are transferring the responsibility. In other words we put the blame on to someone else.

Other people can't make us feel any emotion unless we give them permission. So we allow ourselves to become affected by them and this creates negative reactions. We lose our peace of mind.

STOCKPILE MENTAL RESOURCES

If you constantly fill your store cupboard with mental resources, then when you need to you can dip into them. But if the cupboards are bare then you have nothing to sustain you.

Give yourself praise for the things you do, encouragement to tackle other things and support when you do them.

Be constructive rather than critical. Phrase things more positively, and use optimistic language whenever possible. Look towards finding a solution rather than focusing on the problem. Remember to acknowledge your successes, whether great or small. Most importantly, don't put yourself or other people down.

WRITE IT DOWN

Have you noticed, when you're lying in bed preparing for sleep, how often something comes into your mind that needs your attention or perhaps you have forgotten? Sleeping can now be really difficult.

Having a notebook and pen at the side of the bed means that you can write a note to yourself, even in the dark, which can then relieve you of the worry of trying to remember. Now you really can relax and go to sleep.

> *"When we are at peace, we have within us incredible power to heal and change our world."*
>
> *Diana Cooper*

AUTHOR'S NOTE

I hope you have been inspired to take more time out for yourself to gain peace of mind. It does not matter what form it may take as long as you enjoy what you're doing. Go on spoil yourself.

GOOD IDEA

Remember you have a choice.

FACT

No thought or belief is set in concrete.

CREATING CHANGE

By changing one of the following areas it will enable the other areas to change also because they interact with one another, and are influenced by each other.

> **Environmental Changes and events**

> **Physical Reactions**

> **Thinking Style**

> **Behaviour Change**

> **Mood Changes**

Improve Your Life

MINDFULNESS

Mindfulness is the latest buzzword in the therapy world. Despite this it has been around for a long time in other forms and has many benefits.

The theory behind the word is taking control of your mind rather than allowing your mind to be in control of you.

Sometimes your mind can get in the way.

So it is all about living in the moment and not drifting into the past or the future. So notice when your mind has wandered and bring it back into focus.

This helps to prevent you going into the painful past with regret or recrimination, or 'what if' future, therefore keeping your attention on what is real and not imagined.

There are times when you do need to think to the future, for example when organising or planning.

Being the onlooker to what is going on in your mind can be very informative. So awareness can be helpful to notice the content and form your thoughts take.

Keep in the present and focus on what is happening now, at this very moment.

RELAX

How many of us really relax? Yet relaxation is vitally important to our health and well-being.

Sometimes it can be too easy to say, "There isn't time" or "I feel guilty when I sit down". Maybe you look upon relaxation as doing nothing or boring.

Talking to clients, a lot of people admit that relaxing is either not a priority or something that does not happen due to various reasons. In fact over the years I have found that people say they don't give enough time to themselves. It is so easy to overlook yourself in favour of those other things you tell yourself you need to do.

You owe it to yourself to relax. So every now and then stop what you're doing and take time out for you.

> *Every now and then*
> *it's good to come off the motorway of life*
> *and draw into a lay-by.*

RELAXATION FACTS

Relaxation is something you can learn to do.

Relaxation reduces tension.

Relaxation enables the body to repair and renew itself and reduce biological ageing.

Relaxation improves your physical health and mental state.

Improve Your Life

Relaxation reduces your susceptibility to stress related illnesses.

Relaxation changes your reactions to what is happening around you.

Relaxation improves your ability to deal with pressures and problems.

Relaxation releases beneficial hormones, called endorphins, into the body, which create a feeling of well-being.

Relaxation improves mental alertness, energy levels and sleep.

HOW OTHER PEOPLE RELAX

These are some of the ways that people tell me they relax best.

Having a hug.
Gardening and sitting out in the garden.
Listening to music.
Walking in the countryside.
Taking exercise.
Lying in a dark quiet room.
Reading.
Having a sociable drink with friends.
Having a bath.
Massage.
Sitting in a candle-lit room with nice smells such as aromatherapy oils.
Taking my dog for a walk in lovely surroundings.
Curled up on my bed stroking my cat.

Having a bubbly bath with the lights out and candles lit.
Sitting near water.
Lighting a fire outside at night to look at and listen to with a nice mug of coffee.
Anything to do with outdoors and the sounds of nature; like listening to rain and watching storms.
Sharing tea and biscuits with friends.
A glass of red wine.
Being alone with nothing to do.
Being with my partner when they have no hassle and we can relax.
Enjoying a meal with my partner.
Sitting or lying down in a warm climate reading a book or newspaper.
Going to the gym.
Walking.
Lying in bed when I don't have to get up.
Eating chocolate.
Choosing a cream cake and then having the pleasure of eating it.
Watching the birds in the garden.
My own company.
Chatting to long-distant friends on the phone.
Holidays.
Walking along the beach and paddling in the water.
Sitting and watching the tide come in, especially if the sea is rough.
Buttercups and daisies – a reminder of childhood.
Big mug of hot chocolate.
Stroking my dogs.
Watching a good film.
Watching swans as they glide along the water.
Looking at babies whether human or animal.

NATURE'S NATURAL TRANQUILLISER

Endorphins are opiate-like substances produced by the brain and the pituitary gland. They are a special family of hormones. Doing the things you enjoy induces a feeling of well-being. Whether you are exercising or relaxing, endorphins are released into your system giving you that 'feel good' factor. They also act as the body's own painkillers.

WHY IT IS IMPORTANT TO RELAX AT NIGHT

The body has a natural cycle. Just as in nature when night follows day, so relaxing follows working. The mind and body need to switch off before bedtime. When you have released the day you are prepared for the night.

SWITCH OFF

You wouldn't dream of leaving a car engine running after you have been on a journey. Eventually, you know it would wear out the engine. So it is just as important to switch off your bodily engine after you have used it.

IS IT EASY TO RELAX?

For some people, yes, but for others they have to learn how. You can learn but, like anything, it takes practice. So it is important to set time aside especially for this purpose.

GUILTY FOR SITTING DOWN

It is amazing how many people say they feel guilty for, as they tell me "sitting doing nothing". Far from doing nothing it is just what the body needs. When relaxed, the body is like a limp rubber band rather than a coiled spring ready for action.

NO TIME

Maybe you haven't any time? Yet there is time for other things. What you are actually saying is that you haven't any time for you. Really there should always be time for you. Sometimes all you need is five minutes.

In the chapter entitled 'Love Yourself' I go into more detail on the importance of giving you time.

BORING

People sometimes say, "It's boring". It can be quite difficult at first especially if you aren't familiar with relaxing. Patience is needed. Once you feel the benefits you will be amazed at the difference in how you feel. So learn to enjoy letting go and treating yourself.

STOP WEARING YOURSELF OUT

Your body can only take being under stress for a limited time before it lets you know.

More stress is actually caused by anticipation than by the events themselves. For instance, the fear of being late, missing appointments, not making a sale or being thought a failure.

There is more pressure than ever on women as they juggle to cope with the different areas of their lives. In order to cope, more women are relying on pills or alcohol than ever.

Before the Second World War doctors mainly dealt with the physical effects of stress. Since then they have been dealing with the mental effects as well.

Free the body from unnecessary tension and you can free your mind too.

> *Why are we always rushing?*
> *Where are we going to?*
> *Hurrying our lives away*
> *we're hardly ever still.*
> *Perhaps we ought to stop*
> *and check where we're travelling to.*

HOW THE BODY REACTS TO STRESSFUL SITUATIONS

The body's response is mainly physical. This dates back to 'cave man' times. So although we have evolved in many ways, our reaction to perceived danger hasn't. Fight or flight was nature's way of protecting us. In fact good or bad events (eg excitement and fear) create the same bodily changes.

Adrenaline is released into our bodies bringing about the following changes:

Perspiration increases to cool the body down. The more energy you burn the more you perspire.

The liver releases glucose (blood sugar) into the bloodstream to provide a quick burst of energy for the muscles. The spleen releases stored blood cells and chemicals into the blood stream to thicken blood. (This process allows blood to clot more rapidly if an injury occurs, so bleeding stops more quickly.) The body becomes more resistant to infection.

Pupils dilate to allow more light in and sharpen vision, allowing us to see as much as possible.

The mouth goes dry to avoid adding fluid to the stomach.

Consequently, digestion stops temporarily, allowing more blood to be directed to muscles and brain, sometimes causing the effect we know of as 'butterflies'.

Neck and shoulder muscles tense up to prepare for action. (Tense muscles are more resilient to blows than relaxed muscles.)

Breathing becomes more rapid allowing an increased flow of oxygen to the muscles.

The heart beats faster and blood pressure rises, to provide more fuel and oxygen to parts of the body.

THE EFFECTS OF THESE BODILY CHANGES

They give us extra energy. But if this energy is not released what happens to the excess energy? It is trapped within us. Unless employed in activity or dispelled, this surplus energy may cause physical symptoms.

USE IT OR LOSE IT

By responding to a perceived threat, whether it is panic, fear, anxiety or stress, your body is preparing to do something physical – so muscles are tensed for action. So use it by physical activity or lose it by relaxing.

WHAT HAPPENS IF YOU DON'T RELAX?

The result of the physiological changes and stored up tension can cause one or more of the following:

- Breathlessness and/or palpitations
- Nausea or vomiting
- Dizziness
- Asthma
- A need for alcohol (as opposed to a liking)
- Excessive smoking
- Loss of appetite
- Craving for food
- Insomnia
- Nightmares
- Constant tiredness
- Onset of allergies
- Chronic indigestion
- Nail-biting
- Constipation or diarrhoea
- Finger or foot tapping
- Headaches/migraines
- Anxiety attacks
- Neck or backache
- Ulcers
- Becoming accident-prone
- Eczema or psoriasis

- Addiction to medication/drugs
- Impotence
- High blood pressure
- Anger/violence
- Phobias
- Strokes
- Heart disease
- Cancer

WHAT HAPPENS WHEN YOU DO RELAX?

I find myself in silence
Time becomes a balm
to smooth out all the wrinkles
and produce a state of calm.

When you relax, the following beneficial physiological changes take place:

- Your blood pressure is immediately lowered.
- Your heartbeat slows.
- Muscle tension decreases.
- Your body's demand for oxygen is reduced.
- The flow of blood to your organs and muscles decreases.
- Your natural output of adrenaline is reduced.

During relaxation your primary attention is focused on the physical letting go of tension.

THE INVISIBLE THREAT

Deepak Chopra feels that, as humans we can withstand a great deal of stress from our environment. If pushed too far our stress response will turn on our bodies and begin to create breakdowns both mentally and physically.

Most of the time your cells are occupied with renewal. However, when the brain perceives a threatening situation this process is set aside. A burst of energy is needed to deal with the threat. So the anabolic metabolism that builds the body converts to its opposite catabolic metabolism, which breaks down tissues.

If the perceived threat isn't dealt with you become exhausted, as the body isn't able to return to its normal function of building reserves of tissue and energy.

Under prolonged situations disease can result.

STRESS CAN KILL

Research by physiologists shows, that by giving a mouse very mild electric shocks it arouses a stress response. Each time this happens the mouse's body breaks down a little bit. After a few days of such stress, the mouse will die. An autopsy will show many signs of accelerated ageing. The cause of death was not the external stress but the mouse's reaction – its body killed itself.

WAYS OF RELAXING

There are many ways of relaxing and it is finding out what suits you. As you can see from the earlier list the ways are many and varied. It is your choice. Later on you will find some more ideas.

> *Within you there is a stillness and sanctuary to which you can retreat at any time and be yourself.*
>
> *Siddhartha*
> *Hermann Hesse*

BREATHING

Breathing can reverse the effects of panic.

Deep breathing interrupts messages to the brain and slows the release of adrenaline.

For really effective relaxation, especially during panic attacks or in a state of anxiety, try abdominal breathing.

Place your hands on your abdomen. To begin with, practise the method first before you start counting. As you breathe in push your abdomen out then as you breathe out pull your abdomen in.

Now as you breathe in count up to five. When you breathe out count up to five. Then again breathe in for five but this time breathe out for six. Keeping the breathing in count at five, gradually increase the out breath until you reach the count of ten.

Then allow the breathing to find its own natural rhythm. Continue to breathe gently and slowly. Repeat the above if necessary.

The counting can be adjusted to suit you. For instance you may be able to breathe in for longer, so increase the five to a six or seven. If the out breath is too long up to ten then stop at the number where you are comfortable.

You will find with practice that you can extend the out breath for a longer time.

SILENT SPACE BREATHING

Another beneficial breathing exercise, that is more like a meditation, and clients find it very easy to do, is the following.

There is a silence and peace between breaths.

Sit comfortably and become aware of your breathing. Follow the steady rhythm of breaths as they come in and out.

As you're following the breaths coming in and going out, notice that after you breathe out and before you breathe in again, there is a small gap, a space.

You will gradually become aware of this space after a few breaths.

Almost let yourself go down into that gap, as if you are going down into yourself. Down into the peace that is within you.

Now let each breath take you deeper and let yourself go deeper and deeper into the silence, down into relaxation.

This exercise can be done anywhere and at any appropriate time. It can be for two minutes, ten minutes or twenty minutes, depending on what time you have available.

Even just two minutes can be enough to help you unwind. Therefore it is appropriate to do at work.

This breathing can also be used to help you sleep or when you wake up in the night.

RELAX THOSE MUSCLES

By taking your awareness to different muscle groups you can become aware of any tension you may be holding in any part of your body. Do this in a systematic way starting with your feet and working up towards your head.

When you are driving, check and see if you are gripping the wheel too tightly and relax your grip.

When you are sitting at a desk or in front of a computer, regularly loosen your shoulders. We can hold a lot of tension in our shoulders and the back of our neck.

Also regularly stand up and have a walk around to ease the stiffness from your body.

In fact, no matter what your job get into the habit of regularly checking to see if you are holding tension in any part of your body.

Even if you don't go out to work it is still a good idea to examine your body to make sure it is relaxed, because stress is not just related to work. Home life can also have its fair share of difficulties.

Tense muscles become sore and painful, and can cause physical problems such as headaches, backache, and breathing problems.

Relaxing muscles breaks the cycle of tension – spasm – tension.

When relaxed your body should feel heavy.

TAKE A BREAK

At work perhaps you could go for a walk at lunchtime or sit in your car and have a short nap or listen to relaxing music.

When you are working at home, regularly take a break by again either going for a walk or just stopping what you're doing for a short while.

ROCKING

A mother will naturally rock a crying baby backwards and forwards. If a child is upset and troubled they will very gently rock backwards and forwards.

The rocking motion relaxes the body and stored up tension drains away. No one knows how it works but it does.

So if you want to release accumulated tension rock backwards and forwards, in a rocking chair if you can. The rocking motion will soothe away all those troubles and tension. Tight muscles will relax as the rocking motion loosens them up.

MEDITATION

Meditation, it is said, bridges the inner and outer self; the physical, mental, emotional spiritual self. It is a deeper form of relaxation.

Meditation is like going on a holiday from the outside world in order to take a journey within oneself.

Meditation can be as easy as just listening to your breath going in and out.

There is no right or wrong way only the one that suits you best. Remember practice brings reward.

Before you start, try not to eat or drink for about 20 minutes beforehand. However, leave an hour if you have consumed alcohol.

Find a comfortable place to sit. Make sure your back and head are supported and your hands rest easily in your lap or on the arms of the chair. Or if you prefer you could sit upright in the chair or on the floor.

Spend a few minutes systematically relaxing your body. This will increase the benefit you achieve.

Choose from the following methods:

Close your eyes and concentrate on your breathing. Be aware of the rise and fall of your chest and abdomen. Notice the sound and sensation of the breaths going in and out.

Focus your attention on an object. Really look and study this object as if you have never seen it before.

Use your senses in turn to increase your awareness.

Focus on a candle flame. After a few minutes close your eyes and see this flame in your mind's eye. Become part of the flame.

Repeat a word or sound to yourself over and over again like a mantra.

Experiment with other ways of going within and stilling external thought. Or sometimes you might want to meditate on a particular problem in order to find a solution.

MEDITATION LOWERS BIOLOGICAL AGE

A physiologist called Keith Wallace from University College London researched for his doctorate the effects of meditation on human ageing.

He was able to strongly demonstrate the connection between ageing and stress hormones. Meditation goes to the root of the stress responses, by releasing the tensions that trigger new stress.

Levels of cortisol and adrenaline are often found to be lower in long term meditators and their coping mechanisms have a tendency to be stronger than average.

His research showed that sitting with your eyes closed in meditation induces the nervous system to enter a state of restful alertness. This means the body is deeply relaxed whilst the mind remains in a wakeful state.

Keith Wallace showed that long-term practice indicated that biological age was being reversed. Also reductions were seen in thirteen major health categories including heart disease and cancer.

I'M ILL THEY SAID AND TOOK TO THEIR BED

When Charles Darwin wanted to give himself an excuse to rest in bed for a while he became 'ill'. So also did Florence Nightingale, Marcel Proust and Sigmund Freud as well as many other famous and successful people.

SLEEP

What better way to relax than to sleep, whether it's a doze during the day or a sleep at bedtime? There is something really comforting about going to bed and snuggling down. Comfort is one of our basic instincts.

> *"Sleep is the most natural, universally available remedy against stress and distress that we possess."*
>
> *Jane Lyle*

Soon after falling asleep our body cells begin to divide at a much faster rate than before. This allows almost every part of the body an opportunity to repair and renew itself.

During the deepest stage of conventional sleep high levels of growth hormone are released into the bloodstream. Deep sleep is needed to restore and regenerate our bodies. While dream sleep appears to restore mental harmony.

This is the ultimate in relaxation.

IN CONCLUSION

Our bodies were designed a long time ago. Unfortunately they haven't evolved and changed as quickly as the world about us. So our bodies respond to threats today in the same way that they would have responded thousands of years ago.

If we are to be happy, healthy individuals then relaxation is essential to our lives. By reducing muscle tension, anxiety and stress-related disorders you can improve mental alertness, energy levels and sleep.

It is likely that a relaxed person will live a fuller and longer life. They will cope better with pain and have fewer accidents. They will feel more self-confident and be able to cope more effectively with life.

GOOD IDEA

When a great opportunity looks you in the eye, don't look away, but grab the chance while it is still there.

FACT

You are creating the lens through which you see the world.

HOW TO IMPROVE YOUR SELF IMAGE

Do change the way you to talk about yourself and stop putting yourself or others down.

Do recognise your own qualities and look at changing those you don't like.

Do find the courage to make whatever changes in whatever areas of your life you feel are appropriate.

Do, whilst making these necessary changes, give yourself support and encouragement.

Do be kind to yourself and give yourself some tender loving care.

Do give yourself praise as this will improve your confidence and self esteem.

Do remember you are important so make time for yourself.

Do start to appreciate yourself and acknowledge your achievements, whether great or small.

Do believe in yourself and be willing to be who and what you would like to be.

Do be brave and start to express yourself as this will enhance your self assurance.

For additional help do refer to my book entitled 'Believe in Yourself'.

Finally, do remember to thank yourself for the hard work you are putting in to improve your life as this will also improve your sense of self, and increase your positive feelings of wellbeing.

WEIGHT ISSUES

For some people how they look becomes part of who they are inside and how they feel about themselves.

If you feel that by losing weight it will improve how you think about yourself then go ahead.

Keeping weight stable is all about balance. Balancing what goes in with what goes out.

Weight can also vary depending upon different factors such as bone structure, height and family tendencies.

Weight gain is relative to metabolism and consumption. If you are overweight, and it isn't due to a medical condition, then it means that you have taken in more than you have used up.

One of the reasons diets don't work is that some foods are cut out or restricted so when returning to 'normal' the weight goes back on again. In some instances, because digestion has become sluggish, weight can increase more than before.

The key is to maintain the new healthy habits.

If there is a psychological reason for the weight gain then maybe it would be better to combine losing weight with therapy to deal with the underlying problems.

SOUNDS FAMILIAR?

Do you look in the mirror and dislike what you see?
Do you console yourself by making for the shop, fridge, pantry or cupboard?
Do you tell yourself you deserve a treat?
Maybe you think just a little more won't do any harm?
Perhaps you feel that nobody else cares so why should you?
Do you blame others for encouraging you to eat?
Maybe certain favourite snacks and treats have become your friends over the years?

KNOW YOUR TRIGGERS

Food can be a comfort, reward or consolation and so on. Look for the emotional messages and face them. Don't use food as a substitute.

Eating can become a response to stress, unhappiness or boredom. Gaining weight will just add to your distress and unhappiness and cause you to feel guilty and maybe even depressed.

Enlist the help of a therapist to help you deal with any unresolved emotional problems.

CRAVINGS

Cravings are short lived if you don't give in to them. So distract yourself until the feeling goes. Cravings are conditional responses that seldom last long. They get weaker if you don't indulge them. So become involved in something else that occupies your mind, or go for a walk, phone a friend or relative.

TIPS AND HINTS

Take time over your meal. Eat slowly.
Put your cutlery down between mouthfuls.
Make every meal an occasion. Sit at the table.
Be more aware of how your food looks, smells and tastes.
Take time to savour and enjoy the textures and flavour of your food.
Chew more because digestion begins in the mouth.
Don't eat whilst being involved in doing something else.
Eat only when you are hungry.
Stop eating when you are full.
By focusing on what you are eating you will be aware of the signals that tell you, you are full.
Make sensible choices.
Don't label food as good or bad.
Try eating from a smaller plate.
Bright colours are more desirable so put more of these on your plate.
Remember to maintain fluid levels as thirst can sometimes be mistaken for hunger.
Exercise if you can. Choose which form is more attractive to you, swimming, walking, the gym, classes, dancing, cycling, martial arts and so on.

WHAT ELSE?

Use other resources within this book such as life coaching, goal setting, visualisation and affirmations. Look at my other book Believe in Yourself for more ideas or listen to the cd entitled 'Lose Weight'.

Keep focused on why losing weight is important to you and what the benefits will be. Remind yourself of these facts often and use the magic words –

> PRAISE
> SUPPORT
> ENCOURAGEMENT.

And soon you will accomplish what you set out to achieve.

However, remember that maintenance is the key to keep what you have achieved.

AFFIRMATIONS

Words are powerful and especially the meaning behind them. Emile Coue, a well known French Psychotherapist born in 1857 devised a famous affirmation that is still quoted today.

'Every day, in every way I'm getting better and better.'

Affirmations are sentences constructed in a way that influences and empowers you and gives you a positive approach to yourself and your life.

Perhaps better to keep them short and simple to begin with and then expand as you gain more confidence in putting words together.

Make sure the words are in the present tense, positive and realistic.

Choose uplifting and motivational phrases.

For example –

'I am doing the best I can.'

'My confidence is growing.'

'Each day I see achievement in everything I do.'

'I love the person I am.'

These phrases can be repeated like a mantra throughout the day. Say the words with feeling and meaning. Remember whatever you focus on becomes more real.

VISUALISATION

The nervous system doesn't know the difference between a real or a vividly imagined experience. So this knowledge can be used to your advantage.

As you create the pictures and images of what you want and how you want to be so you increase your motivation to achieve your dreams.

By repeating the visualisation a new neural pathway is created in the brain. Each repetition reinforces this network and helps to strengthen your determination and energy levels.

So create your image, film of something or even have a sense of what you want to achieve.

Make sure it is realistic and achievable.

If you can, put in colour and sound.

See yourself in the picture so you are associated with what is going on.

Keep on developing your images the more practised you become.

Improve Your Life

COLOUR

For those of us lucky enough to be able to see, colour plays a large part in our lives.

For example, a blue sky and bright sunlight lift our spirit.

We use colour in descriptions. Such as off colour when we don't feel well. Green with envy when we're jealous.

Colour also has association in traditions, such as white worn by brides and black worn at funerals.

Seasons affect the colour of the clothes we choose to wear. For instance, we tend to wear darker colours in the winter and lighter, brighter colours in the summer.

Does colour affect your mood?

Colour can now be used for therapy, or to help us psychologically feel better.

In her book on colour, Suzy Chiazzari tells us that red is an energising colour that can help combat negative thoughts and emotions.

Yellow is the colour of the sun, it is cheerful and optimistic. It can aid communication and self-expression.

Green is a stress-relieving, calming colour. It creates a feeling of peace and security.

Blue is tranquil, soothing and encourages creativity. Midnight blue has a particularly relaxing effect.

Notice which colours enhance your sense of well-being or make you feel happier or calmer. Wear the colours that suit you best. So whatever and whichever colours mean the most to you, use them to create the mood that will help you to feel and act in the way you wish.

BE A SUCCESS

So what is success? What does it mean to you? How can it be achieved?

By the time you have finished reading this chapter you will know some of the answers. The rest you will find out for yourself.

In addition you will gain confidence, self esteem and self assurance.

Failure is a word that often goes with success.

Having experienced failure I now realise that the results of my failure were actually successful.

Find out what's holding you back and how to address these issues.

You have the inner resources to achieve whatever challenge you set yourself and inside this book you will find ways to help you succeed.

DEFINITION OF SUCCESS

Below are examples of what other people said when I asked them the question, "What does success mean to you?"

Achieving something you set as a target.
Money.
Success raises your self esteem and you feel good about yourself.
Having a positive mental attitude.

Sense of well-being.
A happy and fulfilling life.
Closely-knit loving family circle.
Doing something I always promised myself I would do but never had the time.
Pulling off a business deal.
Winning.
Sense of recognition.
Attitude of mind.
Ability to perceive success in any situation.
Success is a great motivator.
Being able to interpret life events positively.
Fulfilling a dream.
Good conclusions.
Reaching a goal.
Setting myself a challenge and attaining it.

DICTIONARY DEFINITION

The meaning of success is defined as:

Attainment of wealth, influence or acclaim, fortune, luck and happiness.

YOUR TURN

So now, write down what success means to you.

What do you want to succeed in doing?

What will it mean to achieve your goal/goals?

How will it change your life?

'There is no challenge more challenging than the challenge to improve yourself.'

Michael F Stately

COMMITMENT

The price of success is commitment.

Stephen Joynes, creator of Hoar Cross Hall Spa Resort, says of success,

> *"Success begins when you decide with conviction that you will be successful. Success is achieved through a sustained and committed effort to improve yourself. Success is down to you. Your options and abilities improve unbelievably as you improve yourself."*

WHAT STOPS YOU?

Procrastination
Fear
Self sabotage
Limiting beliefs
Failure
Past mistakes
Worried you can't do it
Etc etc

PROCRASTINATION

'The thief of time'

Procrastination can hold you back and stop you moving forward. So do you justify not making an effort? What excuses are you making?

Cliff Stockamp, a life coaching guru says of excuses –

"An excuse is what happens when you think that something outside you is greater than what is inside you."

"An excuse is a person's refusal to take responsibility for a decision they have already made not to do something."

So be honest with yourself. Is your goal only a dream that you have no real intention of achieving or is it possible that by taking a risk and going for it you can succeed?

You will never know unless you try – so why wait?

FEAR

A psychological fear is always of something that might happen, not of something that is happening now.

It comes in many forms: unease, worry, anxiety, nervousness, tension, dread, phobia and so on.

You are in the here and now, while your mind is in the future.

This creates an anxiety gap because you aren't able to deal with something in the future as it hasn't yet occurred.

You can always cope with the present moment – but not something that is a mind projection.

Yes you can plan and organise events that are occurring in the future but not a 'what if' which is in your imagination and therefore not real.

Fear alarms us that we may not cope or be able to handle things, but if we are honest experience tells us that we can.

Tony Robbins has some good advice he says that –

> Success is the result of good judgement.
> Good judgement is the result of experience.
> Experience is often the result of bad judgement.

SELF SABOTAGE

*'The road is smooth.
Why do you throw rocks before you?'*

Ancient Saying

Do you put yourself down? Are you self critical?
Do you judge yourself and find yourself wanting?

If so, why?

Start to be kind to yourself. You are your own best friend.

Give yourself lots of praise. Devise constructive comments that build you up instead of knocking you down.

Support your dreams and ideas. Create a positive environment for you to grow and develop.

Words can be tools or weapons. So make sure the words you use are tools to enhance your life.

Jean-Paul Sartre once said that, "words are loaded pistols".

LIMITING BELIEFS

'Our only limitations are those which we set up in our mind or permit others to establish for us.'

Napoleon Hill

In answer to people who challenge or criticise say "Thank you for your feedback". Or, "Thank you for your comments".

You are greater than any obstacle that could get in your way. So don't underestimate yourself.

Limiting beliefs are constructions. They are self-imposed therefore they can be changed or replaced.

'The only limits to our realisations of tomorrow will be our doubts of today.'

Franklin D Roosevelt

We reap what we sow. So make sure you are planting the right seeds. Otherwise you could be nurturing a bad harvest.

If your beliefs don't support you - change them.

FAILURE

'Success has a hundred fathers but failure is an orphan.'

Jack Kennedy

Thomas Edison had many failures before he perfected the electric light bulb. He knew that each failure was leading him to ultimate success.

If you never fail – you never learn.

What would have happened if, as a child, you stopped trying to walk or feed yourself because of the times when you didn't succeed?

Failure can sometimes encourage us to be sorry for ourselves and feel a victim. Sympathy is all right if it is brief but unhealthy if sustained.

Enter everything without giving mental activity to the possibility of defeat.

Remember you don't drown falling in the water – you drown staying there.

PAST MISTAKES

Your past does not equal your future.

We have all made mistakes. It is part of the experience of life. There are things I have done or said that I wished I hadn't.

The problem about mulling over past issues is that they tend to bring up negative feelings such as blame, guilt, anger or regret.

We are always experts in retrospect. But we did what we did and said what we said at the time with the knowledge and experience we had then.

Instead look back and ask yourself what you learned from the event. This reframes the experience and gives it a positive outcome.

Also, stop those gremlins in their tracks if they try to remind you. Manage the voices and don't allow them any air-time. If they keep on reminding you, tell them to 'shut up'.

Let the past rest in peace. You have a present and a future to create and these will be built on these past foundations.

WORRIED YOU CAN'T DO IT?

'The future belongs to those who dare.'

When you buy into fear you start doubting. You become worried and anxious. It's not the thing you fear – it is the fear of the thing.

> *'Ships in the harbour are safe – but that's not what ships are built for.'*
>
> Susan Jeffers

In order to avoid pain we stop ourselves doing things. But pain and resistance precede growth. So it is good to give yourself that little push along with lots of encouragement.

The 'ego mind' resists change until the 'I' gets stronger. Give yourself lots of support and praise. This will build up your self esteem.

Stop focusing on the price and cost and look at the benefits. See what you will gain as a result.

So come on, don't wait for the green light –

GO FOR IT NOW.

A STORY OF PERSISTENCE

Anthony Robbins tells the story of Colonel Sanders who created Kentucky Fried Chicken. He didn't fulfil his dream until he was 65 years old.

What prompted him? He had no money, was alone, and had just received his first social security cheque. He started thinking about what he had that was valuable to other people.

His chicken recipe!

What if he sold his recipe and also showed them how to cook it properly? Maybe they would give him a percentage if the recipe generated additional sales.

So he spent two years knocking on restaurant doors. Many people laughed at him.

After each rejection he would tell his story more effectively in order to get better results.

Altogether he had 1009 rejections before he received a `YES'.

The rest, as they say, is history.

What formula did Colonel Sanders use to promote himself and his idea?

He had belief in his product and kept going, never giving up and persisting despite the rejections.

Persistence beats resistance.

Sometimes positive thinking alone isn't enough and other resources have to be brought in to support and enhance you and your project.

Colonel Sanders didn't give up. He would have had many personal barriers to overcome as well as negative comments from other people.

Barriers are created by attitudes of mind that keep you from succeeding. They become a wall that is blocking your progress.

Below are charts for you to fill in which identify these blockages and also the attributes needed to pursue your goal or goals.

BARRIERS TO SUCCESS

eg doubt my ability		

Write on each of the above bricks what is holding you back and stopping you from achieving just what you want.

Now create a path of positive attitudes, thoughts and beliefs that lead you along towards success and the life you want to lead.

	Eg adopt a 'can do' 'will do' attitude	<- Start here
Finish here <-		

GROUND RULES

In his book 'The Tibetan Art of Positive Thinking', Christopher Hansard suggests establishing three ground rules to create any type of success.

1. What you want should be for your ultimate good and benefit.
2. You must be able to carry the creation of what you want through to completion.
3. You must decide how, once your aim is achieved, you will apply it, what you will do with it and how achieving it will change you.

He says "success is not an ultimate in itself but the result of a series of steps made possible by creative thought. Success comes about through thinking it into action."

You need belief in your ambition and not fear the possibility of failure.

Your life must change in order to be successful."

Think about what adjustments are needed that will bring about change and transformation for you.

YOU ARE WHAT YOU THINK

Thoughts are very powerful and are influenced by what you believe. Thoughts and beliefs have the power to influence your behaviour.

Take note of the following:

There are no idle thoughts because every cell in your body thinks. Therefore your body is becoming your thoughts. You become what you think about.

With what thoughts are you feeding your life?

IS IT TRUE?

'A lie unchallenged becomes the truth.'

Feelings may not be facts so stop and ask yourself if what you are feeling is true.

The brain doesn't know the difference between what is real and what is imagined – it only knows what you tell it.

> F false
> E evidence
> A appearing
> R real

There is a big gulf between believing and knowing.

Feelings take up memory. If we repeat something often enough is goes into our long term memory. We think what hasn't happened is real because it is in our memory. This leads to the illusion.

So when you make sweeping statements in the future, stop and ask yourself if it is really true.

Replace or remove that which is harmful and destructive with what is helpful, hopeful and productive. Become a creator not a destroyer.

IMAGINATION

You can now understand how powerful your imagination can be. So rather than creating negative imaginings how much more useful it would be for you to create positive empowering visualisations.

Emile Coue demonstrated the power of imagination. To illustrate he asked people to visualise a plank six inches wide and twenty feet long laid across their living room floor. They would find it easy to walk across.

However, imagine that same plank stretched between two buildings 100 feet in the air!

Would you be as confident now if you had to walk along its length?

Use your imagination to visualise yourself in a situation where everything is going just the way you want it to happen.

Repetition is the key to success. By repeating an image a new neural pathway is created in the brain and so each repetition reinforces the idea. Try it.

SUCCESSFUL ROLE MODEL

Is there someone you would like to emulate or copy?

If so, picture them in your mind's eye.

Think of what it is they exhibit that you want to copy. How do they behave that could benefit you?

Visualise what they do and say. See them demonstrating what it is that you would like to replicate.

Make the picture big, bold, bright and vivid.

Replay this image over and over again.

Now imagine stepping into this body. Feel what they feel. See what they see and hear what they hear. You now have what this person has.

Notice the difference.

Now step out and let these feelings influence how you will behave in the future.

PLAYING TO WIN

Karren Brady was only 23 years old when she took over as Managing Director of Birmingham City Football Club and achieved success in a man's world.

In her book 'Playing to Win' she tells her story and gives advice on how to be successful.

Below are quotations from her book.

"The truth is that ability is what you are capable of, motivation determines what you do and attitude determines how well you do it."

"My business success has been based on a philosophy that, instead of thinking about where we are, we should concentrate on thinking about where we want to be."

"…. No one makes a penny by being negative."

"It is vital to be self-confident and to push towards conclusions without becoming sidetracked."

NEVER TOO OLD

Anne Wood was nearly 50 when she founded her company, Ragdoll production company the creator of the Teletubbies, Rosie and Jim, and Brum amongst others.

J K Rowling struggled for years because the Harry Potter scripts kept being rejected until eventually she sold the first one.

Vera Wang was a figure skater and journalist before beginning her career as a fashion designer at the age of 40. She is now at the top of her profession.

Henry Ford was 45 when he created his Model T car.

Don't let age deter you because there are many other examples of people finding success later in life.

JUST DO IT

Nothing will happen unless you make it happen.

POSITIVE MENTAL ATTITUDE

A positive mental attitude enables you to see the best of a difficult situation. It gives you an optimistic view of life. Rather like the analogy of a glass half full rather than half empty. The contents are the same but it is how you view it that makes the difference.

In his book 'Staying Sane', Dr Raj Persaud states, "In psychology and psychiatry we now conclude that a person's expectations are perhaps among the most revealing things about their personality, and will predict with unerring accuracy what their future holds."

"For example, if you expect good things to happen to you then you will tend to go down a pathway that is very different than if you expect, by and large, bad events to dominate your future. In particular your expectations determine what risks you take, and how persistent you are in the face of adversity."

So how do you remain optimistic and deal with defeat?

CHANGE YOUR PERSPECTIVE

If you change the way you look at something, the things you look at change.

Psychological research reveals that how you explain your past to yourself will determine your expectations in the future.

> *Experience is not what happens to you;*
> *It is what you do with what happens to you.*
>
> *Aldous Huxley*

See the past as a series of lessons and let them teach you what you need to know. Draw this information out and learn from the experience.

> *Stop dwelling on apparent losses in your life, and start looking for the growth and gain that came from them.*
>
> *Catherine Ponder*

So in future ask yourself how you can see an event differently. Is there another way of looking at it? Let go of the past 'Rest in Peace' while you get on with the present and building a future.

COMFORT ZONE

"Behold the turtle. He only makes progress when he sticks his neck out."

Resistance begins the moment you step out of your comfort zone. But by continually stepping out, eventually the uncomfortable becomes comfortable.

If you are uncomfortable it is a sign that you are growing.

So take a risk and step out of your comfort zone. Each time you do, the preceding risks becomes easier.

So set yourself two challenges. Something you can easily achieve and another that will take a little more effort. Take a risk and, with courage, step out of your comfort zone. Go on, you can do it. Tell yourself you can and you will.

Success is not final, failure is not fatal. It's the courage to continue that counts.

Sir Winston Churchill

GOALS

Brian Tracy had the following to say about goals.

"The primary cause of success in life is the ability to set and achieve goals. That's why the people who do not have goals are doomed forever to work for those who do. You either work to achieve your own goals or you work to achieve someone else's goals."

Look at your list of what you want to succeed in doing and choose an item.

> *Obstacles are those frightful things you see when you take your eyes off your goal.*
>
> *Henry Ford*

GOAL SETTING

If you lack motivation this is a good way to start the process. By writing things down it helps you to focus and gives you perspective.

Research has shown that people who set goals are happier, achieve more in their lives and are successful.

Write down a list of what you want to do or achieve.

At the side roughly estimate how long it will take you.

Choose two goals that can be achieved within a month and two that will take longer.

What steps do you need to take to achieve these goals? Write them down. Then break them down into manageable chunks. These then become sub-goals.

For example if you want to have a snack or eat out on your own as a goal then the following would be sub-goals.

> Choose somewhere you like as your starting point.
>
> Go in, taking something to read or look at and just order a drink.
>
> Once this becomes comfortable, include a cake, in addition to the drink.
>
> Again as this becomes easier order lunch or a snack.

Your goal has now been achieved, and you can build up your confidence by going to other eateries.

Remind yourself of the benefits of achieving your goals.

Celebrate and acknowledge each goal reached.

Keep focused and re-write and re-work them if necessary to suit you and your aims.

LIFE COACHING IN BRIEF

Life coaching can be seen as a way of problem solving, resolving issues in a different way, tackling something you've been reluctant to attempt, or finding a new direction or hobby.

Choose something simple to begin with, maybe a small problem you would like sorted, to give you practice.

The steps you take are broken down into the following simple stages.

What is your concern/problem/challenge?

What outcome do you want to achieve?

What can you do? List alternatives.

What could be the results/consequences of your actions?

Make a decision – choose an option.

Now do it. Give yourself support and encouragement along the way.

Evaluate – did it work? Did you have a positive outcome? Do you need to choose another alternative and work through that option?

The item on goal setting can be linked into life coaching.

Improve Your Life

POSITIVELY STRESSED

Stress is what we experience when we are unable to cope with the demands placed upon us by ourselves, others and situations.

When pressure is placed upon us the effect created is stress, which can have either a positive or negative outcome.

A positive outcome of stress would be stimulation. Some people work better this way, when energy is high and the adrenaline is flowing.

If it is a negative outcome then anxiety, worry and fear are the result of pressure being placed upon a person.

Once the demands on us have gone beyond our coping ability, the state of distress can be potentially harmful to both physical and psychological well-being.

Stress is part of life and is relative to the sort of person you are. It can be either:

> Enabling or disabling
> Stimulating or debilitating
> Constructive or destructive

Balance is needed to either reduce the demands or increase coping resources or a mixture of both.

The body's response to stress is mainly physical. Years ago in times of danger man would either fight to protect himself or run away from trouble (flight).

When adrenaline is released into the body our cave man would experience the following changes.

Perspiration increases to cool the body down and burning more energy meant more perspiration. The liver releases glucose to provide a quick burst of energy for the muscles.

The spleen releases stored blood cells and chemicals into the blood stream to thicken blood. This process allows blood to clot more rapidly if an injury occurs, so bleeding stops more quickly. The body becomes more resistant to infection.

Pupils dilate to allow more light in and sharpen vision, allowing us to see as much as possible.

The mouth goes dry to avoid adding fluid to the stomach. Consequently, digestion stops temporarily, allowing more blood to be directed to muscles and brain which sometimes causes 'butterflies'.

Neck and shoulder muscles tense up to prepare for action. Tense muscles are more resilient to blows than relaxed muscles.

Breathing quickens to allow an increased flow of oxygen to the muscles. The heart beats faster and blood pressure rises to provide more fuel and oxygen to parts of the body.

In the modern world we still experience these responses but unlike our predecessors we no longer need the physical survival skills. Reactions are trapped within us and, unable to let go of these physiological changes to release this stored up tension, we experience stress-related symptoms such as the following.

Chronic pupil dilation may bring about vision problems.

Excessive dryness of the mouth may cause difficulty in swallowing.

Frequent interruptions of the digestive process may cause constipation or encourage ulcers.

Chronic muscle tension causes bodily aches and pains, especially a stiff neck or problems with shoulder muscles.

Shallow and rapid breathing can lead to asthma.

Due to increases in blood pressure, hypertension may develop.

THE EFFECTS OF STRESS

An element of stress can be helpful in allowing us to meet the demands and challenges of life but if the levels of stress become greater than we can cope with then problems arise.

We can react in different ways to the demands of stress. What is perceived as stressful to one person can be seen as stimulating to someone else. The difference in perception affects our abilities to cope.

Physical Effects	**Emotional Effects**
Sweating	Anxiety
Palpitations	Fear
Breathlessness	Depression
Faintness	Crying

'Butterflies'	Withdrawal
Tension	Insecurity
Dry mouth	Negativity
Flatulence	Anger
Indigestion	Frustration
Diarrhoea	Paranoia
Cold hands or feet	Inadequacy
Blushing	Frustration
Frequency of passing urine	Hyper sensitive

Thinking Effects	**Behavioural Effects**
Thought blocks	Stuttering
Forgetfulness	Clumsiness
Amnesia	Loss of interest
Lack of concentration	Rejection of others
Putting 'self' down	Insomnia
Self doubt	Aggression
Suppressing feelings	Outbursts/silences
Confusion	Argumentative
Avoidance	Abuse of alcohol/drugs
Difficulty making decisions	Compulsive sex/impotence
Over-intellectualising	Absenteeism
Lack of self belief	Clinginess

WHAT YOU CAN DO TO DEAL WITH STRESS

Sometimes it can be our attitude or perception of the problem that can be the problem, not what appears to be the problem.

By developing coping strategies such as positive thinking and assertiveness, your self image and self confidence will take on more positive aspects and your self assurance will increase.

If put into practice the following ideas will help you deal with your stress.

Active, mental or physical distraction

Take up a new hobby or hobbies
Do some physical exercise such as walking, running, swimming, dancing or going to the gym.
Chores – start and do the things you have always meant to do
Get more involved with people
Be positive whenever possible
Counteract negative thoughts
Think of five times when you have felt good or things have gone well for you or things you have enjoyed which gave you pleasure
Acknowledge your achievements whether big or small
Notice your body language

Self nurturance

Rest – relax more and look at ways of improving sleep
Diet – are there ways it can be improved?
Treats – reward yourself

Emotional expression

Talk to people such as family or friends
Write down how you are feeling
Let it out by seeking professional help
Take up some form of creative expression such as art

Confronting the problem

Thinking it through
Take a positive attitude
Maybe see things from a different perspective
See the person concerned
Talk to the organisation if work related
Can anyone else help you?
How can you help yourself?

STRESS AT WORK

Stress at work can be due to working conditions, the job, your role, relationships, job prospects or domestic conflict.

Use the above to help you resolve the problem.

Take action before the effects become more serious.

Research shows that work stress ages you and damages your health.

So do something now.

Would turning your desk round help, so you are facing a different direction?

Could you put meaningful pictures and photos around your office environment?

Are you allowed to have a plant?

Maybe when you walk out of the premises you wipe your feet before you leave. This mentally leaves work behind.

HAND MEDITATION

Look at your hands. Really focus on them. Feel them. Look at the colour, the lines, the shape, the veins and the nails.

Close your eyes and think about what you use your hands for.

Here is an example –

- To express love
- To carry out work
- To feel textures
- To prepare food
- To touch people and animals
- To show sympathy and support
- To greet people
- To communicate
- To protect yourself

Will you ever take your hands for granted again?

SELF-RATING QUESTIONNAIRE

PROGRESS LOG

Rate yourself from 1 up to 10 (improving)

	Week 1	Week 2	Week 3	Week 4
Confidence				
Self esteem				
Loving self				
Ability to cope				
Stress levels				
Anxiety/worry				
Time for you				
Relaxation				
Comments:				

TO SUMMARISE

Learn to meditate
Meditation can be easier to learn than you think. You can begin to learn using basic techniques and then add on more advanced methods later when you are ready. Meditation relaxes the mind and body, regulates blood pressure, alleviates pain, reduces muscular tension and helps you deal with stress. Regular practice can develop self-discipline, improve personal performance, build self-confidence, increase energy and efficiency, and create a more positive outlook on life. Benefits can be felt almost immediately.

Relax
Relaxation is an important part of life and one that is sadly overlooked by many people. It is through relaxation that the body is able to repair and renew itself. Relaxation changes your reaction to what is happening around you and so enables you to deal with pressures, people and problems. It will help you to cope more effectively with pain and stress. Relaxation is something you can learn to do.

Find a way out of depression
Having depression can seem as if you have entered a dark tunnel that you can't see your way out of. The tunnel can seem like a prison. However there is a way out and you can learn how. People describe how there is a 'stigma' to being described as depressed yet many people will experience depression in their lifetime.

Depression can vary from feeling very down to the more serious clinical conditions. Reactive depression and the one experienced by many people is brought on by life, the events, situations and people that create the feelings of wanting to shut down because we can't deal with them. So look for a way out and take it. Action is the key.

Turn feelings of failure into success
Failure is a perception. It is how we look at something. Just as we can change perceptions, so we can change how we see failure. In reality no one fails because all we do is learn how to do things differently next time. Failure can be due to conditioning. For example if someone, even yourself, keeps saying we are useless or we aren't good enough. Failure can also be due to being critical. Words can be our enemies or our friends. Thoughts can be creative or destructive. Self-talk can be enabling or disabling. We have the power to choose. We all achieve and it is learning to recognise those times when we do. Then you will see success in all areas of your life.

Make positive changes in your life
We all have the power to change and finding the courage enables us to make those changes. Being aware that change is necessary is the first step. Knowing what to change is the second. The resources will be there once you make the decision. There are many changes you can make such as behaviour patterns, attitudes, thought patterns, reactions and habits and so on. Having determination is essential to push them through. Experiencing the improvement will enhance your motivation to continue.

Gain confidence
Confidence is having faith in your ability and believing in yourself. Confidence can be something you feel internally or demonstrate externally. Gaining confidence will help you to bring about the changes you want in your life

Improve Your Life

and enable you to fulfil your potential. By improving the way you think about yourself you will begin to feel more assertive, self assured and more positive. See and feel the difference it makes to your life.

IS THE CARROT BIG ENOUGH?

Start now to begin making those changes that will benefit your life. For change to happen you have to believe it is possible to change.

What do you want to change about your life?
Write them down.

What beliefs do you now have about your life that are holding you back?
Write them down.

What is it costing you to hang on to what isn't right in your life?
Write it down.

What beliefs do you need right now to enable you to make the changes you have identified?
Write them down.

What will be the benefits to you of making these changes?
Write them down.

How will they change your life?
Write it down.

You have the ability so start now. Don't go down the WHEN – THEN ROUTE. What do I mean by that? Some people make comments such as - 'When I have more time then I will …..' or
'When I feel better, then I will ….'

Improve Your Life

You might even think you don't have the ability but I came across a bookmark once that has a true statement which says

'Life is 80% attitude and 20% aptitude'

So get rid of the negative belief that you can't do something that you very much want to do because if it is important to you and your future, you will. Keep persisting and keep focused on what you want and your life will improve.

Just do it ……

A friend who was troubled and weary he knew

would be glad for a lift and needed it too.

On him he would call and see what he could do – tomorrow.

Each morning he stacked up letters he'd write

"More time I'll give to others," he'd say, - "tomorrow".

But the fact is he died and faded from view

and all that was left when the living was through

was a mountain of things he intended to do – tomorrow.

Dr Dale Turners

Take a hint from the above and don't put off taking those important steps that will benefit your future. There is no time like the present.

So make the carrot **BIG** enough and who knows what you will achieve?

After that, remember to 'maintain it in order to retain it'.

INSPIRATIONAL QUOTATIONS

Let these quotations inspire you to achieve your dreams or goals, however big or small they may be.

Every achievement started as an idea.
                                                    Vera Peiffer

What lies behind us and what lies before us are tiny matters, compared to what lies within us.
                                                    Emerson

Your playing small does not serve the world. Who are you not to be great.
                                                    Nelson Mandela

The only place where success comes before work is in the dictionary.
                                                    Vidal Sassoon

All our dreams can come true – if we have the courage to pursue them.
                                                    Walt Disney

The road to success is always under construction.
                                                    Anon

The man who removes a mountain begins by carrying small stones.
                                                    Chinese Proverb

The only thing holding us back from achieving our incredible and unlimited potential is ourselves.

Anon

Don't be distracted by criticism. Remember the only taste of success some people have is when they take a bite out of you.

Zig Ziglar

Fear knocked at the door
Faith answered
No one was there.

Anon

HELP YOURSELF

Self help is a really positive and constructive way of helping yourself to better health, lifestyle and feelings of wellbeing.

You can relax and benefit from cds such as,

> Time for You
> To Help you Sleep
> Relieve your IBS
> Lose Weight
> Be a Success
> Support for the Difficult Times in Life
> Relaxation Therapy

Also available is a published book entitled,

> Believe in Yourself

This book tackles difficult emotional and life-changing issues to help you change and enhance your life.

So there is something for everyone to derive pleasure from and to gain an immense optimism for life and the future.

To find out more and order any of the above please visit, **www.janicejohnson.co.uk**.

Believe in Yourself is also available from Amazon.

BIBLIOGRAPHY

Quantum Healing by Deepak Chopra

A Return to Love by Marianne Williamson

Awaken the Giant Within by Anthony Robbins

Life Coaching by Michael Neenan & Windy Dryden

Chicken Soup for the Soul by

Jack Canfield and Mark Victor Hansen

The Power of Now by Eckhart Tolle

Practising the Power of Now by Eckhart Tolle

Conversations with God Book 3

by Neale Donald Walsh

The Power of Inner Peace by Diana Cooper

Introduction to Buddhism by Geshe Kelsang Gyatso

A Course in Miracles

by Foundation for Inner Peace

How to Meditate by Paul Roland

Colour by Suzy Chiazzari

ABOUT THE AUTHOR

Janice Johnson is a practising Hypnotherapist and Psychotherapist working in private practice. She is also a counsellor and life coach, and has an honours degree in Psychology. By helping people develop their personal awareness and self-image, resolve problems from the past, deal with any behaviour issues, and encourage success, she empowers them to create a positive future.

Over the years Janice has worked with many people and this book brings together the knowledge she gained as a result, also extensive research and personal experience.

Janice has three children and one grandchild. Whilst looking after her family, a home and working full time she studied for seven years to gain her qualifications. Having suffered the loss of close family she also became a bereavement counsellor.

By making life changing decisions herself, she knows that to make any change is hard and even more difficult to put into action. However, the benefits far outweigh the effort.

Her work is fascinating, fulfilling and rewarding, and in the process she has met some wonderful and amazing people.